ENVIRONMENT LAWS: ROLE OF SUPREME COURT AND M.C.MEHTA

VOLUME 2, ISSUE 1 OF BRAIN BOOSTER ARTICLES

MANSI SINGH

Contents

Preface

"Start writing, no matter what. The water does not flow until the faucet is turned on".

- Louis L'Amour

Hundreds of students and professors are contributing their work to Brain Booster Articles, we are here to provide ample information about Law and Contemporary issues. Our aim is to provide a platform for today's generation to express their views and ideas on law and contemporary law.

Publication

This research paper is published in volume 2, issue 1 of Brain Booster Articles

Author

Mansi Singh

CHAPTER ONE

ABSTRACT

The environment concerns are widespread all around the world. Various organisation has taken necessary steps to curb the menace of environmental degradation.This paper is an attempt to highlight the contributions made by the Supreme Court of India and the eminent environment lawyer, M. C. Mehta, in curbing down the degradation of environment. This paper has dealt with the landmark judicial pronouncements and important principles laid down in them. It talks about how judiciary has dealt with Public Interest Litigation under Article 32 of the Constitution. Moreover, how judiciary has balanced its decisions keeping in mind the economic gains and environment protection. It further talks about how judicial activism has commendably played major role in changing the scenario of environment laws

CHAPTER TWO

INTRODUCTION

Environment has always been an important issue, protection of which is not only the duty of human kind but also is necessary for their own survival.The major cause of environmental degradation is human activities. There has been a decline in environment quality due to various reasons such as increase in pollution, defective environmental policies, chemicals, greenhouse gases, global warming, ozone depletion, etc.

After the sixties there has been an inclination in environmental concerns throughout the world. In order to curb the menace and protect the environment decisions were taken at the United Nations Conference on the Human Environment held in Stockholm in June, 1972. India also participated in the conference and discussed various environment concerns.

The Government of India took various measures to curb the peril of environmental degradation, but still there was a strong and urgent need for a proper legislation in that matter. Though there were some laws that either directly or indirectly deals with environment matters, it was expedient to enact a general legislation for environmental protection. Therefore, The Environment (Protection) Bill was passed by both the Houses of Parliament and received the assent of the President on 23rd May, 1986. The Act, The Environment (Protection) Act, 1986, came into force on 19th November 1986.[1]

[1]The Environment (Protection) Act, 1986

CHAPTER THREE

JUDICIAL ACTIVISM

PUBLIC INTEREST LITIGATION

Judicial Activism is a philosophy which holds the view that the courts can go beyond the applicable law to consider broader societal implications of its decisions. Prior to 1980, only the aggrieved party had the privilege to approach the court in his own case. Individuals with no personal interest attachednot permitted to file the suit on behalf of others.

In 1980, Justice P.N. Bhagwati by relaxing on the traditional rule of Locus Standi, introduced Public Interest Litigation. PIL means that a legal action can be taken by the concerned citizens provided that such suit is filed in the larger public interest. It allowed the concerned citizens to move a court even when he is not a party to the case.

Some special features of PIL are stated below:

- Concerned citizen
- Larger public interest
- Expansion of locus standi
- Prima facie case
- To be filed under Article 32 and 226 of the constitution
- Procedure law applicable

ROLE OF JUDICIARY IN PROTECTION OF ENVIRONMENT

The Supreme Court of India has played a vital role in enhancing the environmental laws and has laid down various remarkable principles and doctrines. It has interpreted the constitution and has laid down various judicial pronouncements.

CHAPTER FOUR

JUDICIAL PRONOUNCEMENTS

Subhash Kumar v. State of Bihar[1]

Bench: Justice K.N. Singh and Justice N.D. Ojha.

<u>Facts</u>

The petition was filed by Subhash Kumar under Article 32 of the Constitution by way of public interest litigation for preventing the pollution of the Bokaro river water from the sludge discharged from the washeries of the Tata Iron and Steel Co. Ltd.

The petitioner affirmed that Tata Iron and Steel Co. Ltd works in mining operations in coal mines which is known as West Bokaro Collieries. After the extraction from the mine the coals are graded into pieces. The graded coals are then mixed with other chemicals and later being washed with tons of water.

Allegedly, the surplus waste is discharged into Bokaro river and deposits in the bed of the river. Further, the sledge which gets deposited on the agricultural land affects the fertility of the land. Also, the slurry effluents flow into the Bokaro river resulting in polluting the river and hence, making it unfit for drinking and irrigation purposes. The washeries of the company is a menace for the people living in the vicinity of the river.

<u>Jurisdiction</u>

Article 32 of the constitution is a protector of the Fundamental Rights of the citizen. Therefore, any citizen who has been deprived of their Fundamental Rights can move the court under this Article. With the introduction of PIL any concerned citizen can move the court in any case provided that the suit has larger public interest and no private interest.

Further, right to life under Article 21 of the Constitution also includes Right to live in pollution free environment for enjoyment of life. Therefore, the concerned citizen can move the court under Article 32 in violation of the same.

<u>Petitioner's argument</u>

In spite of several complaints the State of Bihar and State Pollution Control Board did not take any action against the Company.

He relied on Section 17 of The Water (Prevention and Control of Pollution) Act, 1974, in which one of the functions of the State Board is to inspect sewage or trade effluents and to review plans relating to plants set up for the treatment of water and works for the purification thereof.

He also relied upon Section 24 of the Act which states that no person shall knowingly cause or permit any poisonous, noxious or polluting matter to enter into any stream.

Lastly, he claimed relief directing the respondents to take immediate steps to curb the water pollution in Bokaro river.

<u>Respondent's argument</u>

Bihar State Pollution Board

The Board affirmed that the company had applied for sanctions according to Section 25 and 26 of the Act. Before granting company the sanctions the State Board monitored the process of discharge of effluents into the Bokaro river and found that the effluents were not affecting the water quality.

Steps taken by the Board:

1. Direction to the Director of the Collieries to keep a check upon effluents in the Bokaro river.
2. Imposed conditions on the company to install the settling tanks for settlement of solids and rewashing.
3. Regular sampling, testing and communication of results to the Board every month.
4. On petition, the Boards inspected the treatment of effluent on 20th June, 1998. On inspection, except some negligent seepage from the embankment no discharge of effluents into the Bokaro river.
5. Directed the de-sludging of tanks at regular intervals.

Hence, the Board denied the allegations made in the petition.

<u>Judgment</u>

1. Prima facie no good reason to accept the contentions of the petitioner.

2. State Board has carried out his duty and kept a check on the pollution.
3. Present petition is not filed in Public Interest. The petitioner had personal interest as he was an influential businessman who has been purchasing slurry from the respondent company and on refusal to supply large quantity, he started harassing the company.
4. Prayer of interim relief further proves that the petitioner was interested in collecting the slurry from the land of the respondent.
5. Slurry deposited on the company's land belongs to the company and no one can claim their right over it.
6. The PIL filed was frivolous and therefore, the petitioner is liable to compensate all the respondents Rs. 5,000 as costs.

Conclusion

Public Interest Litigation has been introduced in the judiciary to provide justice not only to the citizens who can raise their voice against the injustice but the underprivileged too who because of less legal assistance are not aware of their rights and remedies. As we know that how in Hussainara Khatoon v. State of Bihar[2], Ms. Pushpa Kapila Hingorani became the voice of underprivileged prisoners of Bihar.

PIL strictly prohibits those petitions in which private interest of the citizens are involved. The Apex Court does not entertain such frivolous PIL's and takes strict action, like compensation, for wasting the time of the Supreme Court.

In the present case the petitioner had personal interest. Thus, resulting in dismissal of the suit and imposition of the Compensation on the petitioner.

Rural Litigation and Entitlement Kendra &Ors. v. State of Uttar Pradesh &Ors[3]

Bench: Justice P.N. Bhagwati, Justice A.N.Sen and Justice RanganathMisra.

Facts

The Mussoorie hill chain of Himalayas is famous for its various river flowing from the hills. In 1950, limestone quarrying was done on the hills which involved cutting of trees, mining etc. which led to the degradation of the valley.

Limestone quarrying continued which led to the lack of flora in the valley and therefore, resulted in landslides causing severe damage to human life as well as their agricultural lands. As a result, the Government of Uttar

Pradesh banned and prohibited activities related to mining in 1961. However, the mining operations were resumed after the approval of state legislature for a period of 20 years. After the completion of 20 years there was a demand of renewal of 18 leases. However, the State rejected keeping in mind the environmental degradation. The Allahabad High Court on the contrary allowed such restoration of leases keeping economic gains over environmental concerns.

The Rural Litigation and Entitlement Kendra (RLEK) filed a complaint before the Apex Court in 1983 regarding the concerns over environmental degradation. The Supreme Court took this complaint as a Public Interest Litigation filed under Article 32 of the Constitution. But the complexity of this litigation grew when large number of lessees of lime stone quarries involved in the litigation. The Apex Court reviewed the necessity of mining operations in by appointing Bhargava Committee and further provided with funds for the purpose of restoration in the region.

Petitioner's argument

1. Affecting the human lives living around the valley.
2. Infringement of Article 21 of the Constitution- Right to live in a healthy environment for enjoyment of life.
3. Forests falls under the category of protected list. Therefore, the approval of Central Government is necessary.

Respondent's argument

1. The court has no role to play in the concerned case as per Environment Protection Act, 1986. The Government and the Nation has the authority to decide whether to give preference to economic gains over environmental concerns.
2. Mining activities playa a vital role in enhancing Government's foreign revenue and thus, is in Nation's interest.
3. Banning on mining activities will lead to unemployment.

Timeline of Supreme Court's Judgment[4]
1985 Order by Supreme Court[5]

• In 1985, the Apex court pronounced its first order in the case where it affirmed with the decision of Bhargava Committee by prohibiting on the mining activities falling under C Category. The Supreme Court ordered that all the pending suits concerning the matter will follow the order and shall stand dismissed.

- A Category

Divided into two classes

1. Quarries which fall within the city limits of Mussoorie
2. Quarries which fall outside the city limits of Mussoorie: can be operated if comply with the Mines Act 1952, the Metalliferous Mines Act, 1961 and other relevant statues.

- B Category

Closure of mines in Sahasradhara Block. Other mines were reviewed by another Committee set up by the Court- 'Bandyopadhyay Committee'

1986 Judgment of the Supreme Court

- The Court professed the concerns over environment and how the mining activities contributing in environmental degradation. However, the benefits of mining such as production of special kind of steel could not be overlooked as it helps in economic gains as well.
- The Court has no role to decide whether deposits should be exploited overlooking the environmental concerns or should industrial requirements be satisfied.
- Bandyopadhyay Committee approved only the A Category mines located outside the city limits of Mussoorie.

Final Judgment of the Supreme Court[6]

Mining in some regions of Dehradun Valley violates Forest Conservation Act. Moreover, the Environment Protection Act, 1986 was passed while the suits were pending before the Courts. Keeping the above point in mind the Court professed that every technicality in the procedural laws cannot be taken as a defence in the case where the grave public importance is concerned. The Court further added that the Court would have handled this petition in other way if the petitions were not filed as Public Interest Litigation. Lastly, the Court held that mining activity can be permitted in those regions where it is expedient for the defence of the nation as well as foreign policy.

<u>Key takeaway</u>

1. Right to healthy environment falls under Article 21 Right to Life.
2. Balance between economic gains and environment. Conflict between the two should be reconciled keeping in mind the larger interest of the Nation.
3. The writ petition filed was not inter party dispute but was filed by way of Public Interest Litigation under Article 32 of the Constitution. Therefore, The Environment Protection Act, 1986 cannot take away the jurisdiction of the Court to deal in the matter.
4. Mining activity to be permitted in those regions where it is expedient for the defence of the nation as well as foreign policy.

Vellore Citizens Welfare Forum v. Union of India[7]

Bench: Justice Kuldip Singh, Faizan Uddin and Justice K. Venkataswami.

<u>Facts</u>

Vellore Citizens Welfare Forum filed a Public Interest Litigation under Article 32 of the Constitution. The enormous discharge of untreated effluent by the tanneries in the State of Tamil Nadu is causing pollution in the environment. Further, the untreated effluents being discharged in agricultural fields, waterways, road side and open lands. Moreover, the effluents are being discharge in the Palar River which is the main source of water supply to the residential area. The Tamil Nadu Agricultural University Research Centre, Vellore has discovered that approximately 35,000 hectares of agricultural land has turned either entirely or partially into a barren land andis unfit for cultivation.

<u>Petitoner's argument</u>

1. The water of Palar River has been deteriorated as the untreated effluents discharge in the river which is the main source of water supply in the residential area. Therefore, affecting the human life around the river.
2. The petitioner further alleged that the chrome tanning process in tanneries involves 170 chemicals like sodium chloride, sodium sulphate, chlorium sulphate, fat, liquor, ammonia and lime etc. the effluents have further deterioratedphysio chemical properties of the soil and have contaminated groundwater by percolation.

3. An independent survey conducted by Peace Members i.e., NGO shown that 350 wells out of 467 which are used for drinking and irrigation has been contaminated.

Respondent's argument

1. The Ministry of Environment and Forests has not yet provided the models for inland surface water release for Total Dissolved Solids (TDS).

Judgment

1. Imposed fine of Rs. 10,000 to all the tanneries for causing pollution which is to be deposited at the District Collector's Office.
2. Compensation to be paid under 'Environment Protection Fund'.
3. Establishment of 'Green Bench' under the supervision of Madras High Court to further investigate in the matter.
4. Even though the leather industry contributes to economic gains does not provide them the shield to degrade the environment and causing menace to the health of citizen of the country.
5. Rejected the traditional concept of development and ecology. Supported 'Sustainable Development'.
6. Directed Central Government to take immediate actions under Environment Act to curb down the pollution.
7. The standards laid down by NEERI to be maintained by all the tanneries and the Stae of Tamil Nadu.

Key Takeaway

1. The tanneries should not be allowed to operate at the cost of lakhs of people
2. Precautionary and polluter pays principle has been held to be a sound principle and has been accepted by the law.
3. A 21 of Constitution provides citizen the Right to live in a pollution free environment.
4. Sustainable Development is the part of the process of remediation of damaged environment.

Indian Council for Environment Legal Action v. Union of India and Ors[1]

Bench: Justice B.P.Jeevan Reddy and Justice B.N Kirpal.

Facts

An environmentalist organisation filed the writ petition to throw light on the sufferings of people living in the vicinity of chemical industrial plants in India. In Udaipur there is a small village known as Bichhri and to its north there is a major industrial establishment, Hindi Zinc Limited. The chemicals like Oleum and Single Super Sulphate produced in Hindustan Argo Chemicals Limited caused serious threat to the environment. The toxic untreated effluents caused due to 'H' acid were allowed to be released in the open and therefore, is a menace to the environment. Further, the wells turned dark in colour and are unfit to drink.

In order to protest the villagers in unison revolted which results in imposition of Section 144 of CrPC by the District Magistrate of the area and thus, resulting in closure of Silver Chemicals in January 1989.

The present Public Interest Litigation was filed in August 1989 complaining of the above situation and a proper remedial action for the same.

Petitioner's argument

1. The 'H' acid produced by Silver Chemicals and Jyoti Chemicals has polluted the environment posing grave threat to the environment as well to the citizens and cattle living in the vicinity of the industries.
2. The water in wells turned into dark colour and is unfit for drinking and irrigation purposes. Further, the soil has also been polluted.

Respondent's argument

1. Questioned the jurisdiction of the Supreme Court by relying on Article 12 and stated that since the respondent are private companies the writ petition do not lie against them.
2. No action taken on other countries engaging in 'H' acid.
3. Reports of RSPCB are unreliable and defective.
4. A complete stoppage of use of 'H' acid by all the Respondents.
5. Suggested the establishment by way of legislation of proper environment courts.

<u>Judgment</u>

1. Rejected the contention of the Respondent stating that even if the private companies do not fall under Article 12 if the Supreme Court finds that the Government or any other Authority responsible by law has not taken appropriate action which is jeopardising the right of citizens then the Court has the all the right to intervene in the matter.
2. The writ petition has been file as a Public Interest Litigation under Article 32 by the villagers of the affected area.
3. Rejected the contention of the Respondent stating that even in the absence of opportunity of cross examine the experts, the report submitted by the bodies cannot be declared as unreliable or defective.
4. As per the reports by National Environment Engineering Research Institute by the Central team and Rajasthan PCB, the respondents were held accountable for all the loss caused by the pollution.
5. Relying upon the decision in Oleum Gas Leak case, the court stated that it is the sole responsibility of the respondent to indemnify all the individuals who have been affected by the hazardous activity carried out by them.
6. Lastly, ordered the closure of all the chemical plant and machinery causing pollution the area.

<u>Key takeaway</u>

1. Relied on principle of Absolute Liability and Polluter Pays principle.
2. Court can intervene in the matter even if the respondent is the private company and do not fall under Article 12 of the Constitution when the appropriate authorities failed to take necessary actions.
3. Absolute liability is not subject to any exceptions laid down in Rylands v. Fetcher.

[1] (1996)3 SCC 212
[1] (1991) 1 SCC 598
[2] (1980) 1 SCC 98
[3] (1985) 2 SCC431
[4]AnubhaChatrurvedi, Legal Wires, Case Study: Rural Litigation and Entitlement Kendra v. State of Uttar Pradesh, Available at https://legal-wires.com/case-study/case-study-rural-litigation-and-entitlement-kendra-

v-state-of-uttar-pradesh/(last visited on March 25, 2022)
    [5] (1985) 2 SCC 431
    [6]1989 Supp (1) SCC 504
    [7](1996) 5 SCC 467

CHAPTER FIVE

JUDICIAL REMEDIES

In India Judicial remedies are divided into two

1. Tortious Remedies
2. Statutory Remedies

Tortious Remedies:
Strict Liability: Principle of strict liability was enunciated in Rylands v. Fetcher. It was held that if the defendant possesses anything that is hazardous or inherently dangerous, he will be liable for any damage caused by such possession, even when the defendant was diligent enough to prevent the harm.

Injunction: Granted by the court to prevent any further damage. The provision related to perpetual Injunction is provided under section 37-42 of the Specific Relief Act, 1963.

Trespass: Wrongful interference into the property of other. Trespass under tort does not fall under criminal act but Indian Penal Code has recognised the same and punishes for criminal trespass under Sec 447.

Nuisance: The act of pestering the enjoyment of any person. It is further divided in two types of Private and Public Nuisance. In the former the defendant interferes in the enjoyment of one's land and in the latter interference in the general public right.

Negligence: Failure to exercise care in the situation where a reasonably prudent person would have exercised.

Statutory Remedies:
Environment(Protection) Act, 1986- **Section 19**
Criminal Procedure Code, 1973- **Section 133**
Indian Penal Code, 1860- **Section 268**

CONTRIBUTIONS OF M.C. MEHTA IN PROTECTION OF ENVIRONMENT

<u>JUDICIAL PRONOUNCEMENTS</u>

M.C. Mehta v. Union of India[1]

(OLEUM GAS LEAK CASE)

Bench: Then Chief Justice P.N. Bhagwati, Justice RanganathMisra, Justcie G.L. Oza, Justice M.M.Dutt and Justice K.N. Singh.

<u>Facts</u>

M.C. Mehta was an environmentalist and social activist who filed Public Interest Litigation under Article 32 of the Constitution. This case is famously known as *'Oleum gas leak case'*. This incident occurred after 1year of Bhopal Gas tragedy.Shriram's Food and Fertiliser Factory, was situated in Kirti Nagar, Delhi, produced hard technical oil and glycerine soaps. M.C. Mehta filed writ petition for the closure and relocation of Shriram Caustic Chlorine and Sulphuric Acid Plant. The Delhi administration appointed an expert committee, the Manmohan Singh Committee, to supervise and inspect the operations of the factory.

On 4th and 6th December, 1985, during the pendency of the suit the oleum gas leaked from one of its units causing menace to local residents. It was found that on 4th December, the reason of leakage was the bursting of the tank containing oleum gas and on 6th December the oleum gas escaped from the pipe's joint resulting in wave of claims for compensation.

Further, the Supreme Court appointed many other committees namely, Agarwal Committee, Nilay Choudhary Committee and Expert Committee.

After the recommendations made by the Committee the Supreme Court allowed the plant to restart its capacity and work only if it follows the recommendations made by the committee.

Other issues involving substantial question of law were referred to the larger bench i.e., constitutional bench.

<u>Issues</u>

1. Whether the industries which pose a menace to the local residents should be permitted to continue their operation in the area?
2. How the Court should determine the compensation and liability in such cases?
3. Whether after the permission is granted, there is a necessity to establish regulating mechanism for regulation in such areas.
4. Whether Article 32 can extend its blanket in such cases?

5. Whether principle of Absolute Liability or the principle involve in Ryland v. Fetcher should be permitted?
6. Whether 'Shriram' industries fall under the meaning of 'State' as per Article 12 of the Constitution?

Judgment

1. Justice P.N. Bhagwati stated that the menace to the local residents living near the factories can be reduced by adhering to the measures recommended by the Committee. The industries to be positioned in the area where the residents are less vulnerable.
2. Permanent closure of the industry would lead to unemployment. Therefore, the court ordered that the factory should adhere to 11 conditions in order to operate in the area.
3. Following are the conditions: -

1. To create a safety committee for the welfare of the employees
2. In order to check whether the industry is being operated in compliance with the Water and Air Act, the Central Board should appoint an inspector.
3. The industry should herald the consequences and the proper treatment of chlorine.
4. Proper training via audio visual services should be provided to employees for their safety.
5. In case of gas leak, install the loudspeakers to alert the residents living in the vicinity of the industry.
6. Proper equipment like helmet and belts to be used for safety.
7. In case of any death or injury, Shriram factories will held 'personally liable' for paying compensation.

Key takeaway

1. The court held that all exceptions set out in the Rylands v. Fetcher case are not applicable to hazardous industries.
2. If the Court finds that there is menace to the fundamental rights, the power under Article 32 will not be limited to preventive actions only but will also be applicable to remedial acts.

3. Supreme Court acted in the capacity of parliamentary body by contending that the principle of Absolute Liability should be used.

M.C. Mehta v. Union of India[2]
(TAJ TRAPEZIUM CASE)
Bench: Justice Kuldip Singh, and Justice Faizan Uddin
<u>Facts</u>

Petitioner alleged that the major reason behind the monument's (Taj) degradation are the chemical and hazardous industries and refinery at Mathura. The refinery emits Sulphur Dioxide which when combines with oxygen forms sulphuric acid called as 'Acid Rain' resulting in degradation of the white marble. Further, the emission was polluting the environment around Taj Trapezium Zone. Thus, the white marble was turning in yellow and black in colour.

The petitioner has therefore urged the Supreme Court to take necessary and expedient action to prevent the degradation of the monument which is the pride of India.

An Expert Committee was established which submitted its report namely 'Report on Environmental Impact of Mathura Refinery' by Varadharajan Committee stating that there is presence of Sulphur Dioxide in the atmosphere causing the pollution. According to the Committee the possible sources of pollution were the Power Plants using coal, small industries and Railway Shunting Yard. The Committee recommended immediate action to be taken to curb the degradation by no further permission to be granted to any new small industries which can cause further pollution in the north west of Taj Mahal. Further, gave directions to relocate the small industries in south- east of Agra. Lastly, the Committee recommended that no large industries should be established in the region before assessing the implications of that industry on the monument.

The Central Board for the Prevention and Control of Water Pollution, in order to curb the pollution, published a report under the title "Inventory and Assessment of Pollution Emission in and around Agra and Mathura region". The report suggested some measures and statistics to deal with the matter. Further, The Nation Environment Engineering Research Institute (NEERI) gave an "Overview Report" in relation to the status of pollution in Taj Mahal in 1990.

<u>Judgment</u>

1. Taj is not only a heritage but also an industry as it attracts lot of tourists. Hence, it is a source of income for the country. Therefore, preservation of the monument should be done immediately.
2. The court heard the case for three years and stated that the Trapezium Zone of Taj was being polluted resulting in degradation of the monument.
3. The emission forms the industries is discolouring the white marbles of the monument.
4. The purpose of this litigation is to curb the pollution and simultaneously encourage the development of the industry.
5. Focus to be placed on 'Sustainable Development'.
6. The onus of proof is to be placed on the industry to show that there is emission of any hazardous effluents which can have adverse effect on the environment and thus degrade the monument.
7. Relocation of industries falling in Taj Trapezium Zone only if the industry fails to substitute coal with natural gas.

Key takeaway

1. Reliance placed on Precautionary Principle.
2. State Government and the Statutory Authorities took initiative to implement some environment measures.
3. Relied on the principle of polluter pays, which was enunciated in Vellore Citizens Welfare Forum v. Union of India, which extends the liability to not only pay compensation but also restore the damage caused to the environment.

M.C. Mehta v. Union of India[3]
(KANPUR TANNERIES CASE)
Bench: Justice E.S. Venkatarmaiah and Justice K.N. Singh
Facts

The petitioner is an active social work who has filed the petition under Article 32 of the Constitution as Public Interest Litigation in the nature of mandamus to restrain the Respondents to discharge hazardous effluents from the tanneries Jajmua, Kanpur into the river Ganga until they install treatment plants to curb down the pollution in the river. The Ganga River is the holy river of the country, the Hindus worship the river and it is the source of survival for many living in the vicinity of it.

Petitioner's argument

1. The effluents releasing from the tanneries are hazardous and thus, causing damage to the holy river, Ganga.
2. Affecting the people living in the vicinity of the holy river.
3. The Unemployment which will result from the closure of the industries is minute as compared to public health.
4. Installation of treatment plants is necessary to curb down the pollution

Respondent's argument

1. Effluents from the tanneries are not being directly released into the river. The effluents discharge in municipality therefore, it is the duty and responsibility og the municipality to not let the effluent mix up in the river.
2. Installation of treatment plants is to expensive.
3. Closure of factory will lead to unemployment in masses.

Judgment

1. No dispute that the discharge of effluents from the tanneries are the cause of degradation of the holy river as well as the aquatic animals in the river.
2. The industries cannot escape the liability by stating that the effluents discharges form the municipal sewerage.
3. No steps taken as per Water (Prevention and Control of Pollution) Act and the Environment (Protection) Act, in order to curb and eliminate the discharge of trade effluents into the holy river.
4. It is impossible for the industries to install the large treatment plants in short notice, therefore, the least they can do is to install the primary plans.
5. The financial capacity of the industries will not be taken into consideration while installing the primary plants.
6. No permission to continue the operations of the industries until installation of primary plants.
7. Directions to install the primary plants within six months.

Key takeaway

1. Initially, in the preliminary hearing the Supreme Court published the gist of petition in the newspaper and circulated in the regions of northern India and called all the industries falling under the area of Ganga River to give reasons as to why the directions should not be imposed on them.
2. The Supreme Court also stated the importance of Article 48 A and 51 A of the Constitution.
3. The end of practice of throwing away the corpses in the river.

M.C. Mehta v. Union of India[1]

Bench: Justice Kuldip Singh and Justice S. Saghir Ahmad

Facts

The Indian Express that Kamal Nath (Respondent) has direct links with the private company namely, Span Motels Private Limited, which runs a resort. The same company also runs a club namely, Span Club. The club embodies Kamal Nath dream of having a house on the Bank of Beas in the shadow of snow capped Zanskar Range. It was alleged that in 1990 the club was built after the encroachment upon 27.12 bighas of land, including substantial forest land. The regularisation was done when Mr. Kamal Nath was the Minister of Environment and Forest. Later, the it was found that the swollen beas submerged into the Span Club and the adjoining lawns. Therefore, to change the course of rivert the company was rolling the bulldozers and earth mover. Resulting, in causing flood and damage of property worth Rs. 105 Crores.

Petitioner's argument

1. Kamal Nath, Minister of Environment and Forest, was behind the regularising of the forest land encroachment performed by Span Motels.
2. He had personal business interest in the property.
3. Majority of shares of Span Motel were owned by the family of Kamal Nath.
4. The encroachment caused floods in the region and therefore, has disturbed the ecological balance.
5. Violation of Article 21 and 51 a (g) of the Constitution.

Respondent's argument

1. Contended that he had no rights, title or interest in the property namely, 'Span Resorts' owned by 'Span Motels Private Limited'. Therefore,

cannot be placed as a respondent. Later, the counsel of Kamal Nath stated that the fact that Mr. Kamal Nath's family holds almost all the shares of the Motel Company is not disputed.

2. The allegations made in the press report is false, exaggerated and was made to taint his reputation.

3. No malafide intention to change the course of river. It was done to prevent soil erosion.

4. Permission to carry out the construction work was granted by Divisional Forest Officer subject to the condition that the Department won't be liable to pay any amount for the construction.

<u>Judgment</u>

1. The Supreme Court applied the 'Doctrine of the Public Trust', which sets out the freedom to enjoy the natural resources like air, water, sea and forest and thus, can never be subject to private ownership.

2. The resolution of the problem in given case is on the legislature and not the courts. But in the absence of legislation, the doctrine of public trust does not allow any individual to own the natural resources.

3. The large area of bank of River Beas which is a part of protected forest was given on the lease to the Motel Company. Therefore, it was held that the lease transactions are in patent breach of the trust held by the State Government.

4. Span Motels are liable to pay compensation for changing the course of the river.

5. The Court gave directions to NEERI to inspect the land and determine the cost to reverse the damaged caused.

6. Further, the Court barred the Span Motel to discharge any trade effluent into the River Beas.

<u>Key Takeaway</u>

1. Application of Public Trust Doctrine

2. The Government and the appropriate authorities were not responsible to take necessary action against the exploitation of the natural resource.

3. The Court rightly upheld the environment justice.

[1] (1997) 1 SCC 388

[1] (1986) 2 SCC 176
[2] (1997)2 SCC 353
[3] (1987) 4 SCC 463

CHAPTER SIX

PRINCIPLES AND DOCTRINES LAID DOWN BY SUPREME COURT OF INDIA

1. **Public Trust Doctrine**

In M.C. Mehta v. Kamal Nath, the Supreme Court laid down this principle which rests that the natural resources like air, water, forest and sea can never be owned privately by any individual.

2. Doctrine of Absolute Liability

In Union Carbide Corporation v. Union of India, the Supreme Court laid down this principle which rests that where any enterprise has dangerous/ hazardous substance in possession or is carrying out any harmful activity resulting in any mishap either to the human kind or environment will be held liable to pay the compensation irrespective of the fact that the respondent was not negligent. Hence, the Supreme Court laid down the Absolute liability with no exceptions.

3. **Doctrine of Sustainable Development**

According to this principle the resources on theearth are limited therefore, the Government should meet the needs of present without comprising with the needs of future generations. The Government should introduce such policies that will meet the needs of both current and future generations. The court should strike a balance between development and environment.

4. Polluter Pays Principle

In Vellore Citizens Welfare Forum v. Union of India, the Supreme Court held that polluter pays principle is an essential part of Sustainable Development. According to this principle the polluting party will not only pay the damage caused to the environment but also take necessary steps to restore the environment.

5. Precautionary Principle

In Vellore Citizens Welfare Forum v. Union of India, the Supreme Court held that precautionary principle is also essential part of Sustainable Development. According to this principle the Government should assume that there will be pollution in certain areas and should assume its severity and impact on the environment. Keeping in mind the above assumption the Government should take precautionary measures to curb and limit the possible degradation of environment.

CHAPTER SEVEN

CONCLUSION

The Supreme Court of India had done a commendable job in bringing out the important and necessary changes in environment laws. They have struck the perfect balance between economic growth and environment development. Moreover, placed an emphasis on environment protection over economic growth when the economic growth results in severe environment degradation. The Court has rightly placed the doctrines and principles in their pronouncements and therefore formed prodigious judicial precedent. The court heard the petitions filed under Article 32 of the Constitution by way of Public Interest Litigation.

It could be rightly said that the Supreme Court played major role in protecting the environment by interpreting the Constitution of India. Apart from the doctrines and principles, the Court has expanded Article 21 of the Constitution by including the right to enjoyment of pollution free water and air for full enjoyment of life.

M.C. Mehta was an environment lawyer as well social activist who has filed plethora of Public Interest Litigation with the sole purpose of protecting the environment. His contributions to the environment are nonpareil. The petitions filed by him in the court of law resulted in remarkable and landmark judgments in environment laws. He filed many petitions as Public Interest Litigation under Article 32 of the Constitution.

In *Oleum gas leak case*, the court dealt with the important question of compensation to be paid to the victims affected by the leakage from the factory. Therefore, resulted in the introduction of the doctrine of Absolute liability with no exceptions.

In *Taj Trapezium case*, the court relied on the precautionary principle as well as on the principle of polluter pays.Therefore, sets out principle that the accused should not only pay the compensation but also should take necessary steps to curb down pollution and restore the environment.

In *Ganga Pollution case,* the court placed importance on Article 48 A and 51 A of the Environment (Protection) Act, 1986. Further enunciated that economic growth cannot continue at the cost of environment. Expedient to take necessary steps to curb down the environment degradation.

In *Kamal Nath case*, the court placed an importance on Public Trust Doctrine.

LIVING WAYSIDE(S)